Hertfordshire

2 5 JUN 2008
18 FEB 2009

9/12

Please renew/re

So that you
please c

st

R   23   37373
                                           7378

STEAM WAGONS
IN FOCUS

by John Crawley

PUBLISHED BY
JOHN CRAWLEY LTD, TURVEY, BEDFORDSHIRE

©JOHN CRAWLEY LTD 1984

First published in 1984 by
John Crawley Limited
Field House, Turvey
Bedfordshire MK43 8DU

Printed in Great Britain by
AB Printers Limited, Leicester

ISBN 0 9508046 2 2

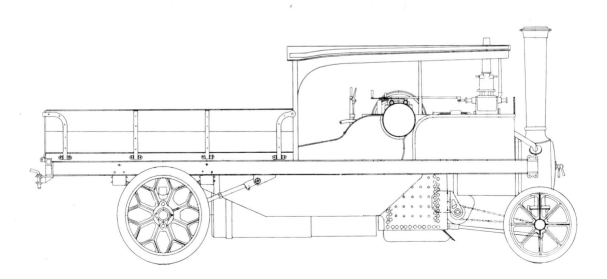

FOREWORD

by J.E. Foden

How very pleased I was to receive the invitation to write the foreword to this book, which has brought the names of the smaller makers of steam wagons flooding back, giving me immense nostalgic enjoyment, and enabling me to recall many events which seemed to have faded with time.

I well remember my first visit to Elworth Works at the age of nine, when my father took me through the erecting shops and explained to me all that was happening. Looking back I realise that this was my baptism into the commercial vehicle business in which I was to become increasingly involved over the next sixty-two years until my retirement in 1972.

The steam vehicle in all its forms has long endeared itself to the user and provided an intimacy that I believe is not achieved with any other form of propulsion. That transformation from a cold piece of machinery as soon as the fire is well alight; that spreading warmth as she comes to life; that wonderful smell of hot oil and the crackling and spitting that goes on in the firebox are all part of the magic that is the steam engine. From such moments a relationship is formed that stays with one for ever and the fascination of steam has claimed yet another victim.

This fascination ruled me from the time of that escorted tour of the erecting shops with my father, and very soon I was making unlawful visits on a Saturday afternoon to the traction shop, a large building that housed the new traction engines awaiting collection or delivery. Together with my brother, a friend and a supply of dry wood, I would slip into the shop by a somewhat devious route and set about steaming a couple of the engines, having great fun getting them to tick over, although we made no effort to move them around.

I am afraid to say that from this simple pleasure the activities escalated and it was not long before we were accompanying brother Bill, who was eight years my senior, into the garage, that large building where the new steam wagons were awaiting delivery.

A game developed in which we steamed up a wagon, which brother Bill would then drive down the length of the floor as fast as possible before stopping as close to the end doors as he could judge. Having taken bets on the distance between his front wheels and the door, measurements would then be made before proclaiming the winner. Needless to say Bill, endeavouring to show his ability to stop within inches of the doors, eventually misjudged his stopping power and went out through the end into the yard beyond. Fortunately time has dimmed the certain retribution that was inflicted upon us, but I can well remember father eyeing Bill very sternly and saying, 'Bill, that is not the way we drive a wagon, that is the way we dismantle them'!

People today can visit traction engine rallies and see steam wagons perform but unfortunately, with one or two exceptions, only examples from the more prolific builders have survived. The great appeal of this book is to be able to see so many wagons whilst they were going about their normal work, often kept gleaming by their proud owners, but just as often in a work-worn condition, far removed from that of the finely renovated vehicles appearing at modern rallies.

John Crawley is to be congratulated for producing another first class volume to add to the series which makes available so many old photographs whose survival is now assured, and I was particularly interested in the Foden selection as regrettably so few photographs have survived within my family.

From close examination of the pictures it is possible to learn a lot about the conditions that were experienced by the earlier road haulage contractors and I can thoroughly recommend this book not only to those fascinated by steam but to all interested in the history of mechanical road transport. Elsewhere in this volume the author says, 'Here is the evolution of the steam wagon in pictures,' a statement with which I enthusiastically concur.

E. Foden

9th April 1984

INTRODUCTION

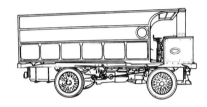

Towards the end of the last century, transportation, whether by ship or by train, was thoroughly steam-oriented: there had even been an unsuccessful steam aeroplane. At the end of a railway journey, a traveller could take a horse cab or a horse bus, or, in a larger town or city, a steam tram.

Problems began with the increasing traffic in goods, which depended on collection or delivery by horse and cart, or, in the case of very heavy goods, by steam tractor and trailer. In the countryside the problem was particularly acute, despite an extensive railway system bearing no resemblance to the truncated network we know today. There were many villages and hamlets well outside the daily range of horse and cart, and the need of a self-propelled vehicle for heavy goods work became more and more apparent.

Many small engineering firms saw the opportunities and tried building prototypes, only to find that performance was not good enough for the design to be marketable, while others produced efficient wagons that could not be manufactured economically. They overstretched themselves financially and were forced to retire, licking their wounds. Out of this industrial mayhem emerged a number of stronger firms like the Lancashire Steam Wagon Company (which became the Leyland Motor Company, and after various changes of name and fortunes is still with us today) and Fodens Ltd, who only recently have been forced to sell out by the harsh economic conditions of the late seventies.

Around the turn of the century there were two types of steam wagon; the overtype, owing its design to the traction engine, in which the cylinder and motion were on top of the boiler, and the undertype in which the engine was more often than not totally enclosed and mounted beneath the chassis.

Fodens Ltd, of Sandbach, Cheshire were the largest builders of overtype wagons, although, in the late twenties, market trends forced them to move into the undertype field. Before they could establish the same kind of reputation as they had for overtypes, however, they had abandoned steam power for the internal combustion engine.

In 1906 Alley and MacLellan, a Glasgow engineering firm, entered the market with an undertype wagon which they had been developing over the previous two years, and by 1915 their business had grown so much that they needed to build a new factory. This they did at Shrewsbury where, two years later they changed their name to Sentinel Waggon Works Ltd, using their own characteristic spelling with a double 'g' in waggon. Their original waggon remained in production with few modifications until 1922 when a new range was introduced. They continued building improved ranges until 1938, and in 1950 there was a minor revival when they received an order for 100 waggons from the Argentine. This proved to be the finale of their steam waggon building, and they too went over to the internal combustion engine before having to yield to the economic climate. The latter two manufacturers each built more wagons than all the other makers together.

As in my previous book, machines that are in preservation today are marked ■ after the engine number; and the building date given is usually the date on which the wagon became available to the sales department for delivery or collection.

To the many contributors of photographs, which are individually acknowledged, I must offer my sincere thanks, and also to Alan Duke for his continuing support and ever-forthcoming answers to my many queries.

Finally, no greater honour could befall the author of a book on steam wagons than to have the foreword written by Ted Foden, a man not only with a great reputation in the commercial vehicle business, but also one who actually served his time building steam wagons. To Mr Ted, as he was affectionately known throughout the Foden works, I am most grateful for his generosity in setting his seal of approval on this my third book on steam road vehicles.

John Crawley

1. William Allchin Ltd built 41 Three ton wagons. This overtype No 228, registration No NH 1680 was the fifteenth, built in June 1915 and sold to Henry Hamp & Sons of Northampton. By September 1925 she had been scrapped. *(author's collection)*

2. Allchin 3 ton overtype wagon No 287, Registration No NH 1780 was built in November 1915 and sold to J. Cragg of Romsey in Hampshire. *(courtesy P. Smart)*

3. Allchin 5 ton overtype tipping wagon No 1189, Registration No NH 3019 was built in July 1920 for the Northampton Corporation. This photograph shows her in the depot yard on 5th October 1946 by which time the Corporation had changed its title to County Borough of Northampton. She was No 2 in their fleet.

(courtesy B.D. Stoyel)

4. Allchin 5 ton overtype wagon No 1196, Registration No NH 3209 was built in September 1920 and sold to George B. Davies of Ludlow, Salop. She had finished her working days by 1933 and had been sold for scrap. *(courtesy P. Smart)*

5. Atkinson 6 ton undertype wagon No 162, Registration No CK 3165 was built in December 1919 and delivered to Daniel Thwaites & Co Ltd of Blackburn. On 28th December 1922 she was totally wrecked after crashing through the side of Holt Mill Bridge and had been scrapped by March 1923. *(courtesy J.W. Cole)*

6. Atkinson 6 ton undertype wagon No 482, Registration No CK 3679, was built in June 1925 and sold to Edward Hankins, haulage contractor of Preston in Lancashire. In September of the following year she was sold to Shephard & Hough Ltd of Stirchley, and was last licenced in December 1930. *(author's collection)*

7. Aveling & Porter overtype wagons belonging to Haulage Ltd of Walworth, London pose for the camera. On the left is No 7594, Registration No D 7133, built in January 1912 and given their fleet No 7. She was sold in 1916 to W.E. Chivers & Sons Ltd, of Devizes. On the right is No 7409, Registration No D 6499, built in July 1911 and given their fleet No 1. She was sold in 1915 to T. Redburn & Son of Brimsdown, Middlesex.

(courtesy J.L. Middlemiss)

8. Aveling & Porter 4 ton overtype wagon No 7916, Registration No D 9168, was built in March 1913 and sold to F. Bowles & Sons of Cardiff. In 1916 she was purchased by the South Hetton Coal Co Ltd of County Durham.

(courtesy J.L. Middlemiss)

9. Aveling & Porter 4 ton overtype wagon No 8494, Registration No KT 4035 was built in January 1915 and sold to Peak Frean & Co Ltd of Bermondsey, London. The abbreviated name is possibly a wartime economy.

(courtesy B.D. Stoyel)

10.   Aveling & Porter type FGR overtype wagon No 8949, Registration No KN 1583 was built in November 1918 and sold to Stratton Gentry & Company Ltd of Kew Bridge, London. She was later acquired by George J. Cockerell & Company of London where she became No 6 in their fleet.   *(courtesy Charrington Ltd)*

11.   Aveling & Porter 4 ton overtype wagon No 9075, Registration No KN 5159 was built in February 1920 and delivered to G.P, Tatner & Co Ltd of Dartford, Kent with whom she spent all of her working life.

(courtesy B.D. Stoyel)

12 & 13.   Two views of the Berry undertype 5 ton wagon, Registration No F 536 which was built *circa* 1902 by A.W. Berry of Port Lane Works, Colchester. She was sold to the Colchester Brewery Co Ltd but worked for only a few years before being put aside due to continual trouble with the boiler.   *(courtesy R.G. Pratt)*

14 & 15. Two photographs of undertype wagons manufactured by Bretherton & Bryan. L.C. Bryan was apprenticed to Davey Paxman & Co Ltd of Colchester, but he left them and after a short spell with Napiers set up in business with F.J. Bretherton at premises in Grange Road, Willesden Green, London. The wagon was designed by Frank Bretherton and, no doubt as a result of L.C. Bryan's previous association with the Colchester firm, they undertook the building of the vehicles on their behalf, although it is not certain that they were the only builders. The first wagon was to have made its debut at Cordingley's 10th Annual Motor Show held at London's Islington Agricultural Hall in March 1905, but completion was not to be rushed and it was not ready until some two weeks later. Around this time problems were being experienced with the production of suitable wheels and it is interesting to note that the cast wheels in the lower photograph were imported from Krupps of Essen.   *(courtesy R.G. Pratt)*

16. Bretherton & Bryan's first undertype wagon, Registration No A 9619 was supplied in 1905 to H.H. Finch, wine and spirit dealer of Marylebone, London who worked her until 1912 when she was sold to White Jacoby & Co Ltd of Camden Town. *(courtesy R.G. Pratt)*

17. Peter Brotherhood Ltd, the well known Peterborough Engineering Company, was all set to enter the commercial vehicle field in 1921 when threatened litigation from the Yorkshire Steam Wagon Company Ltd over the design of the boiler caused Brotherhoods to cancel their plans. The similarity to the Yorkshire boiler can be seen in this photograph of the Brotherhood undertype tipping wagon which spent its life as works transport. *(courtesy Peter Brotherhood Ltd)*

(courtesy S. Mustill)

18 & 19.   After cancelling their plans to market a range of undertype wagons, Peter Brotherhood Ltd were left with three vehicles on hand. The first, Registration No FL 2571 went to Schweppes in London who were 90% owned by the Brotherhood family at that time. The second vehicle, FL 2603 and the tipping wagon, which was never licenced for use outside the factory spent their lives as works transport until the early 1930s. *(Above)* The tipper and FL 2603 in the works yard and *(below)* FL 2603 with her driver in a street near the factory.

(B.D Stoyel)

20 & 21.   Two views of the Bristol undertype 4 ton chain driven wagon, Registration No AE-B3, built *circa* 1904 by the Bristol Carriage & Wagon Co Ltd. At the time these photographs were taken the wagon was on demonstration and her subsequent owners are not recorded. It is thought that total production of this make did not exceed six vehicles.   *(author's collection)*

22 & 23.   Burrell 5 ton overtype wagon No 3358, Registration No AH 077 was built in February 1912 and sold to Malcolm Atwell of Churchill in Somerset. For some reason it would seem that the owners were not satisfied with her for after only two months they sold her to F.P. Ford & Sons of Shipham in Somerset. By January 1930 she had been scrapped. This wagon was fitted with double chain final drive, whereby the rear wheels were mounted on a dead axle each being driven by its own chain, the chain cases being clearly discernable in the two illustrations. The differential was fitted on the countershaft and could be easily locked by the driver.   *(author's collection)*

24.   Burrell 5 ton overtype wagon No 3513, Registration No AH 0159 was built in October 1913 and sold to H.W. Archer of Spennymoor, Co Durham. By 1920 she had been sold to showman A. Newsome of Darlington and by 1926 was with her last owners, Adams of Stockton-on-Tees. This wagon was fitted with double chain drive and was one of a later batch made with the chassis frame curved in an arc to go under the gear guards before resuming the horizontal. This photograph shows her making a beer delivery to the Salvin Arms public house in Spennymoor.   *(author's collection)*

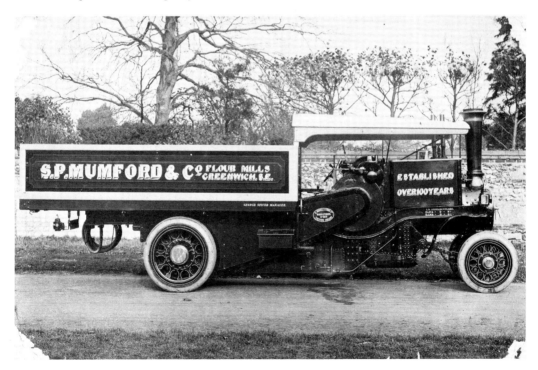

25.   Burrell 5 ton overtype wagon No 3623, Registration No AH 0219, was built in November 1914 and sold to S.P. Mumford & Co of Greenwich, London. The curved side frame on this later version of the double chain drive wagon can easily be seen in this view.   *(author's collection)*

26.   Burrell 5 ton overtype
wagon No 3877, Registration
No SX 1569 was built in
February 1923 and sold to Kent
Bros of Linlithgow, Scotland.
They named her *Maid o' the
Mountains*, fitting a brass
nameplate on the gear side of
the body just forward of the
rear wheel. In March 1925 she
was sold to R.G. Howling &
Sons of Ingoldisthorpe, Norfolk
who used her for the rest of
her working life.

(author's collection)

27.   Burrell 5 ton overtype
wagon No 3954, Registration
No WT 273 was built in
August 1923 and sold to
George Essem & Sons of Balby,
Doncaster. By mid 1929 she
had been sold to R.S. Pye of
Emswell, West Suffolk who
scrapped her in 1934.
This wagon was built with
single chain final drive with
the differential on the live
rear axle.

(author's collection)

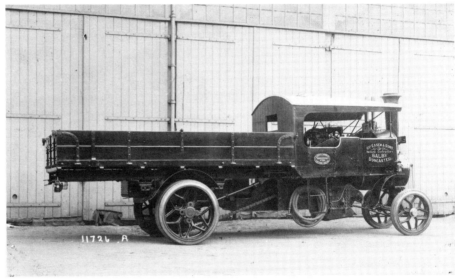

28.   Burrell 6 ton overtype
wagon No 4003, Registration
No FJ 3722 was built in June
1925 and sold to J. Hancock &
Son of Exeter. She had two
subsequent owners,
G.H. German & Co Ltd also of
Exeter and finally Ralph
Dumma & Son of Jedburgh,
Scotland who last licenced her
in September 1931.

(author's collection)

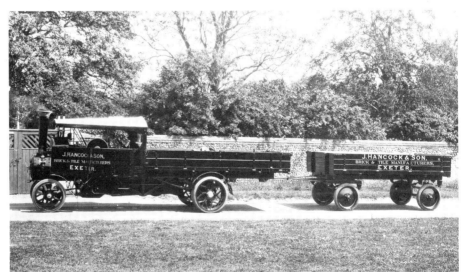

29. Burrell 5 ton overtype wagon No 4008, Registration No PW 5936 was built in July 1925 and sold to H. Kay Ltd of Horsham where she spent the whole of her working life as a wagon (see below, plate 30)

(author's collection)

30. The remains of Burrell overtype wagon No 4008 pictured here driving a saw bench near Folly Hill, Horsham. Her owners, H. Kay Ltd of Horsham, had converted her into a portable engine and in this form she was to survive into the early 1950s, probably making her the last survivor of this make of vehicle.

(author's collection)

31, 32 & 33. Burrell 6 ton
overtype wagon No 4027 fitted
with 3-way tipping body was
built in November 1925 and
exhibited on Burrell's stand at
the Smithfield Show in
December. In January 1926 she
was sold to John Hardie & Sons
of Bo'ness, West Lothian,
Scotland where she spent the
whole of her working life.
Fitted with single chain drive
and Ackerman steering, she
represented the final design of
wagon made by this well
known firm.
The three photographs shown
on this page well illustrate the
tipping versatility of the
Burrell: the normal position,
side tipped (either side to
choice) and end tipped.

(author's collection)

34.   Burrell 6 ton overtype wagon No 4078, Registration No SM 6697 was built in January 1927. It is probable that this wagon was built for stock as she was Burrell's entry in the *Commercial Motor* Magazine 1000 Mile Trial which commenced on 9th November 1927 and finished at the Olympia Exhibition Hall in London on 17th November. A single chain driven wagon with Ackerman steering, she is seen in this view with her advertising boards fitted ready to leave Thetford to take part in the trial. Some time after this event she was sold to John Charlton & Sons of Dumfries in Scotland.   *(author's collection)*

35.   Carter 5 ton undertype wagon designed by Frank Carter and built by his company, Carter's Steam Wagon Company, in 1905 at their works in Bridgefield Street, Oakenrod, Rochdale, Lancashire. Unlike most wagons of the day, the Carter had a vertical compound engine mounted in the cab behind the vertical boiler. Whilst it had been on the market since the previous year its London debut was delayed until Cordingley's 1906 Motor Show at the Agricultural Hall, Islington, where a 5 ton tipping wagon was also exhibited.
(courtesy B.D. Stoyel)

36. Clayton & Shuttleworth 5 ton overtype wagon No 47136, Registration No FE 1591, built in April 1915 and sold to Turner & Son Ltd of Nottingham. She had three other owners during her life, Barsby & Co of Nottingham, in 1920 William Burgess of Stockport, Cheshire and finally Jeremiah Carley of Chatteris, Ely. In this picture she is taking water at Daybrook, Nottingham. *(courtesy F.H. Gillford)*

37. Clayton & Shuttleworth 5 ton overtype tipping wagon No 48274, Registration No FE 2660 was built in July 1919 and sold to Mangham Bros of Rotherham, Yorkshire. In this photograph she is seen on Clayton & Shuttleworth's stand at the Royal Agricultural Show at Cardiff in 1919.

(courtesy T.B. Paisley)

38. Clayton & Shuttleworth 5 ton overtype tipping wagon No 48410, Registration No FE 904 was built in December 1919 and sold to S.T. Rosbotham of Bickerstaffe, Lancashire, where she spent the whole of her working life.

(courtesy B.D. Stoyel)

39. Clayton & Shuttleworth 5 ton overtype wagon seen on test at Lincoln prior to handing over to the War Department. The registration numbers are 'trade plates' which were used until the vehicle was delivered.

(courtesy A.J. Winkfield)

40. Clayton & Shuttleworth 5 ton overtype wagon doing duty with the Army Service Corps in France in the Spring of 1919. On the wagon are W. Walken, Mate Bricknell and J.J. Jones. *(courtesy T.B. Paisley)*

41.   Clayton 5 ton overtype
tipping wagon believed to be
No T1033, Registration No
FE 3970 was built in December
1920 against an order from
Hendon Urban District Council.
After only five years work she
was fitted with a new boiler
which lasted until she was
sold, presumably for scrap, in
1935.
(courtesy B.D. Stoyel)

42.   Clayton 6/7 ton overtype
wagon No T1136 ■,
Registration No VG 1825, was
built in June 1929 and sold to
Norwich Corporation. In 1948
they sold her to Max Cremer of
Cromer in Norfolk and later
she was acquired by
G.T. Cushing of Thursford,
where she is now in
preservation. This type of
wagon was introduced by
Claytons at the 1926 Smithfield
Show at the Royal Agricultural
Hall in London.
(author's collection)

43.   Clayton 6/7 ton overtype
wagon No T1182, Registration
No VG 259 photographed in
Norwich on 28th August 1934.
Built in January 1928 she was
sold to Lacey & Lincoln Ltd of
Norwich who used her until
she was laid aside in 1935.
(courtesy B.D. Stoyel)

44 & 45. Coulthard 5 ton undertype wagon, thought to be No 406, Registration No BL 249, which was built in January 1902 and sold to James Dewe of Burghfield Mills, Reading. In August 1908 she received a new Registration No BL 03. In these two photographs she is seen well loaded with her proud owner, prior to his men setting out on a delivery journey.   *(courtesy P.R. Barker)*

46.   Coulthard 5 ton undertype wagon, Registration No CKC 4, was built *circa* 1905 and is photographed in the ownership of W. Anderson, Sons & Hedley of Newcastle-on-Tyne.   *(courtesy B.D. Stoyel)*

47.   Coulthard 5 ton undertype wagon, Registration No CK 420 was built in September 1905 and sold to the North Eastern Railway Co where she became their fleet No 8. She survived well into LNER days but was out of use by 1928.   *(courtesy K. Hoole)*

48.   Danks 5 ton overtype wagon No 106, Registration No CW 1531, was built in January 1916 and sold to John Riley & Sons Ltd of Hapton, Lancashire. In January 1920 they sold her to Woodhead Bros of Wortley in the West Riding of Yorkshire and she was last licenced by them in September 1927. She is seen here with her driver, George Bargh, in the works yard at Wortley.   *(courtesy Leeds Traction Engine Club)*

49.   An early undertype wagon built by Jesse Ellis & Co Ltd of Maidstone, Kent. The first vehicle built by this company appeared at the Royal Show held in Birmingham in 1898. This picture was taken outside the works and shows Jesse Ellis who was rather partial to being photographed with any of his engines. The company went into liquidation on 30th April 1907.   *(courtesy B.D. Stoyel)*

50.   Ellis 5 ton undertype wagon, Registration No D 330, was built in 1903 and sold to J. Batchelor & Son of Little Chart, Kent. In 1914 she was sold to Charles Hooker of Loose, Kent and her last owner was Henry Farmiloe of Great Chart, Kent who bought her in 1918. It is not known how long she survived working for him. Again Jesse Ellis proudly presents himself in the background.
(courtesy B.D. Stoyel)

51.   Ellis 5 ton undertype wagon, Registration No D 337 was built in 1903 by Jesse Ellis & Co Ltd of Maidstone, Kent and sold to Style & Winch of the Medway Brewery, Maidstone.
(courtesy B.D. Stoyel)

52.   Ellis 5 ton undertype wagon, Registration No D 646 was built in 1904 and sold to Dartford Brewery Co Ltd. After approximately twelve months she was returned to the makers where she remained until sold in 1907 to Joseph G. Ford of Wokingham, Berkshire, where she worked until laid aside in 1914.
(courtesy B.D. Stoyel)

53. 5 ton overtype wagon No 536, registration No B2030. Built by Fodens Ltd at Elsworth Works, Sandbach, Cheshire, in May 1902 and sold to W.R. Allen of Widnes, Lancashire. She was only the fifth wagon to be made by the firm. Later she was sold to Smith Bros of Worksop, Nottinghamshire, where she remained for the rest of her working life. In this delightful picture members of Widnes Town Council are being transported through the town to view the decorations on the day prior to the Coronation of H.M. King Edward VII in 1902. The driver of the wagon was James Woodward. *(courtesy J.W. Cole)*

54. Foden 5 ton overtype wagon No 538, Registration No D 676, was built in May 1902 for Thomas Wood & Sons of Swanley, Kent. Sometime prior to 1917 she was sold to Charles Hooker of Boughton Monchelsea, Kent where she remained for the rest of her life. In this photograph she is seen collecting tomato baskets from Hewets the basket makers of Swanley. Thomas Raymond Wood, in the bowler hat, is standing by the front wheel, whilst Master Thomas Henry Wood, aged six, is seen on the footplate. *(courtesy E. Wood)*

55.   Foden 5 ton overtype tipping wagon No 739, Registration No AU 67 was built in April 1904 and sold to the Stoney Lane Brick Company of Eastwood, Nottinghamshire. She was later rebuilt as a standard 5 ton wagon and sold to John E. Whiting of Owleston, Sheffield. In September 1910 she was acquired by Frederick Ray of Bedford where she worked until last licenced in December 1924. She appears to have a mechanically operated tipping gear as well as provision for hand cranking on both sides of the body. The drive to the lifting gear is by means of a shaft across the entrance to the cab the other end of which is driven off a friction disc on the end of the crankshaft. *(author's collection)*

56.   Foden 4 ton overtype wagon No 958, Registration No M 928, was built in August 1905 and sold to Samuel Smith of Sheffield. In 1912 she was acquired by dealers, William Reynolds of Bedford, who sold her the same year to J.W. Seddon of Platt Bridge, Whiston in Lancashire. Five years later she was sold to J. Welsby of Rainhill, Lancashire, wher she was last licenced in January 1927. *(author's collection)*

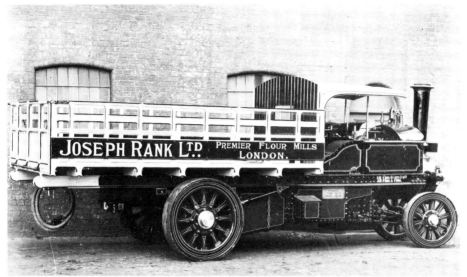

57. Foden overtype wagon No 1128, Registration No M 1185, was built in July 1906 and sold to Joseph Rank Ltd, of London where she became their fleet No 11. In February 1926 she was returned to Fodens, presumably in part exchange against a new vehicle. The same month they sold her to Hall Davidson of Ewell in Surrey who were her last recorded owners.
(author's collection)

58. Foden overtype wagon No 1154, Registration No M 1277, was built in August 1906 and sold to William Pritchard of Caernarvon, Wales. In 1919 she was sold to Bolton Corporation (Waterworks Department) who used her until November 1926 when she was sold to Thomas Ratcliffe (Bacup) Ltd.
(author's collection)

59. Foden 4 ton overtype wagon No 1278, Registration No M 1430 was built in March 1907 and sold to Giles & Harrap of Merthyr Tydfil, Wales. In 1933 she was sold to Slagmag Paving Co Ltd of Cardiff, but it would seem that something went wrong with her that would have cost too much to repair as whe was not licenced after July 1933.
(author's collection)

60. Foden 4 ton overtype wagon No 1342, Registration No M 1526, built in May 1907 and sold to Frank White of Newton Abbot, Devon where she spent her working life until she was scrapped in 1930. This illustration is an advertising postcard sent out by Frank White in the course of his business. It is interesting to see that the printers have lettered the original photograph with white ink and then re-photographed for the purpose of making the printing plate from which to produce the postcard. However, it would seem that the lettering was given to a junior for 'Hauling Contractor' should surely have been 'haulage' and 'Newton Abbott' should only have one 't' in Abbot. *(courtesy B.D. Stoyel)*

61. Foden 4 ton overtype wagon No 1346, Registration No M 1603, was built in June 1907 and sold to Cannon & Gaze Ltd of Erith, Kent, where she became No 5 in their fleet. The whole of her working life was spent with this firm until she was sold in 1925 for scrapping to W. White of Erith, Kent. In this photograph, taken in November 1907, she has run out of control at Crayford Bridge demolishing a police box in the process. *(courtesy Bexley London Library)*

62. Foden 4 ton overtype wagon No 1879, Registration No M 2320 was built in June 1909 and sold to William Gardham & Sons of Staines, Middlesex. In 1914 she was bought by the Penrith District Road Carrying Company Ltd of Glenridding, who last licenced her in January 1926. This photograph shows her still lingering in their yard at Glenridding in September 1935. *(courtesy B.D. Stoyel)*

63. Foden 4 ton overtype wagon No 2926, Registration No M 3695, was built in March 1912 and sold to Jolly & Sons of Stonham, Kent. In 1918 she was sold to the Hextable & District Haulage Company Ltd of Kent but by the beginning of 1922 she had been acquired by H.W. Clarke & Son Ltd of Erith, Kent who used her until she was cut up for scrap in 1926. *(courtesy R.G. Pratt)*

64. Foden 3 ton overtype tipping wagon No 4330, Registration No X 3697, was built in February 1914 and sold to Northumberland County Council where she became their fleet No 16. She spent all of her working life with this authority. *(courtesy B.D. Stoyel)*

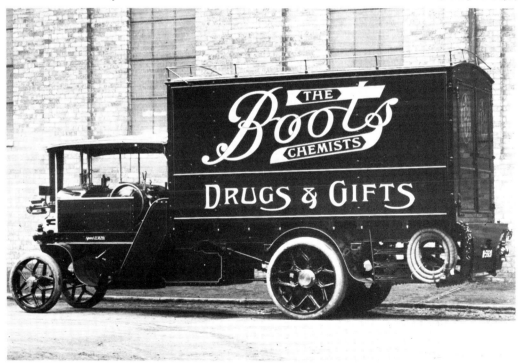

65. Foden 3 ton overtype wagon No 4358, Registration No M 5928 was built in April 1914 and sold to Boots Pure Drug Co Ltd of Nottingham. After nine years with this company she was sold to E. A. Foley of Bourne in Lincolnshire and a year later, 1924, she went to Fred Palmer of Boston. She had one more owner after this and survived into the 1930s. *(author's collection)*

66. Foden 3 ton overtype wagon No 4394, Registration No M 6029, was built in June 1914 and sold to Richard Pool of Fleet in Hampshire. By the time she was scrapped in 1932 she had had seven different owners.

(author's collection)

67. Foden 4 ton overtype wagon No 6082, Registration No M 8289, was built in February 1916 and sold to Thomas Rigby & Sons Ltd of Frodsham, Liverpool. In 1921 she was sold to James Hall & Sons of Warrington where she is seen in this photograph taken *circa* 1926. They last licenced her in October 1931.

(courtesy J.R. Scott)

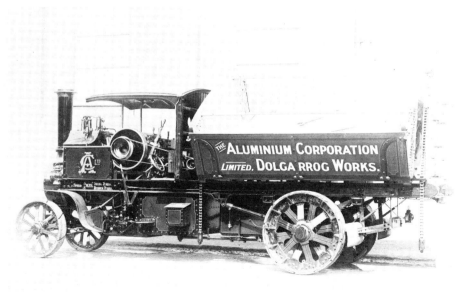

68. Foden 4 ton overtype tipping wagon No 6382, Registration No M 8713 (later changed to MA 1730), was built in July 1916 and sold to the Aluminium Corporation Ltd of Dolgarrog, Caernarvon in Wales. Later she was acquired by the Pengwern & Gwydyr Quarries Ltd, of Trefriw, Caernarvon, who were her last recorded owners. In this photograph she is seen demonstrating the 3-way tipping body which is actuated by belt drive from the flywheel.

(author's collection)

69, 70 & 71. Foden 4 ton overtype tipping wagon No 6858, Registration No M 9134, was built in May 1917 for Salford Corporation Highways Department. She was fitted with a crane capable of lifting 1¼ tons which was operated by belt drive from the flywheel. The wagon body tipping mechanism was still hand operated by means of one or two crank handles which could be operated from either side or both together. At a later unrecorded date she was sold to the Kent County Council but in October 1930 was taken back by Fodens, perhaps in part exchange for another vehicle. They sold her to Gordon Hill of Crewe, her last recorded owner.

(author's collection)

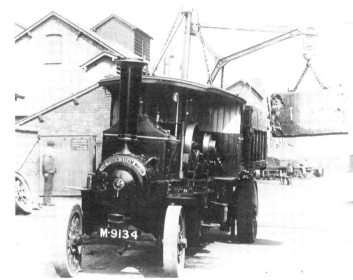

72.   Foden 4 ton overtype wagon No 7890, Registration No M 9591, was built in February 1918 and sold to Robertson Bros of Woking, Surrey. In 1921 she was bought by George Baker of Southampton who sold her in July 1922 to the Isleworth Brewery Co Ltd of Middlesex where she became their fleet No 18. She is seen making a routine delivery for the brewery *circa* 1935 and about two years later in 1937, was sold for scrapping.
(courtesy B.D. Stoyel)

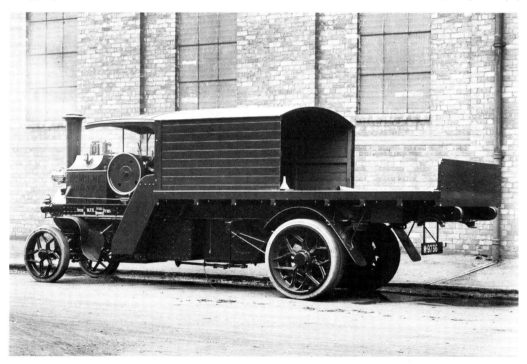

73.   Foden 4 ton overtype wagon No 8172, Registration No M 9736, was built in July 1918 for William Milne of Glasgow. In 1928 she was sold to George Halliday & Sons of Palnackie-by-Dailbeathe, Kirkcudbright where she was still at work in 1933.
(author's collection)

74.   Foden 3 ton overtype tipping wagon No 8220, Registration No M 9729, was built in July 1918 and sold to Renwick, Wilton & Co Ltd of Torquay. By 1923 she was with E. Pratt & Son of Southend-on-Sea and in January 1931 was sold to W.G. Smoothy & Sons of Rochford, Essex who worked her until 1935 when they sold her for scrap to S. McKay of Thundersley.   *(author's collection)*

75.   Foden 5 ton overtype wagon No 8808, Registration No MA 528, was built in May 1919 and sold to W. Everard & Son Ltd of Leicester. In 1929 she sold to W.H. Mason & Son of Burton-on-Trent and in 1933 to Fryers Garage of Uttoxeter, her last owner. In this view she is seen ready for delivery at Foden's works.

(author's collection)

76. Foden 5 ton overtype chassis No 9252, Registration No MA 1412, was built in September 1919 for Hooke & Son of Peterborough, Northamptonshire. In 1932 she was sold to A.J. Pledger & Co of Stamford, Lincolnshire, who in turn sold her in 1934 to William Wells of Huntingdon who last licenced her in May 1935. This photograph shows her ready for despatch from the factory. *(author's collection)*

77. A Foden 5 ton overtype wagon belonging to Cannon & Gaze Ltd of Erith, Kent. No further details are recorded but it would appear that it has run backwards out of control, possibly due to the broken chain laying on the road which is the cause of the discussion taking place. *(courtesy Bexley, London Libraries)*

78.   Foden 6 ton overtype wagon No 11112 was built in 1923 and used as a company demonstrator until sold on 1st April 1925 to Barlow, Phillips & Co of Yeovil, Somerset, when she was first licenced and received the Registration No YB 1734. In this photograph she has dropped through a grating outside the 'Popular Cafe', one cannot but feel that the driver's name for this cafe would have been different. *(courtesy J.L. Middlemiss)*

79.   Foden 6 ton overtype wagon No 11500, Registration No TP 408, was built in November 1924 and sold to John Kiln of Cosham, Hampshire. John Kiln is seen in the centre of this picture whilst taking delivery of his new vehicle, with his manager on his right, and Jim Abbiss, Foden's driver to his left. *(author's collection)*

80. Foden 6 ton overtype wagon No 11632, Registration No CH 4518, was built in November 1924 and sold to Unwin Sowter Ltd of Derby. She is seen here in the ownership of J. & R. Hutchinson Ltd of Nottingham and was later acquired by Joseph Stockdale of East Markham where she spent the rest of her working life.
(courtesy F.H. Gillford)

81. Foden 6 ton overtype tipping wagon No 12162, Registration No PR 6723, was built in April 1926 and sold to G. Maidment of Parkstone, Dorset, where she spent the whole of her working life. *(courtesy J.H. Hobbs)*

82. Foden 6 ton overtype wagon No 12364 ■, Registration No TW 4207, was built in July 1926 and sold to Edward B. Devenish of Rayleigh, Essex. After twice changing owners she was bought by Taroads Ltd of Hatfield, Hertfordshire and this photograph shows her with Northern Taroads at their Kendal depot in July 1952 fitted with tar spraying equipment. After two further changes of ownership, Woods of Yeadon in February 1959 and Charrington, Hargreaves of Leyburn in January 1962, she was sold for preservation in October 1963. *(courtesy P.N. Williams)*

83. Foden 6 ton overtype wagon No 13044, Registration No MP 5938, was built in July 1928 and sold to E. & J. Fountain of Uxbridge, Middlesex. She was later purchased by Taroads Ltd of Hatfield, Hertfordshire and eventually transferred to their Northern depot at Kendal where she was last licenced in February 1952. She is seen at work tar spraying near Appleby on 13th June 1951. *(courtesy R.G. Pratt)*

84.   Foden six wheel overtype tipping wagon No 13052, Registration No TU 9942, was built in January 1929 and used as a company demonstration vehicle although she was hired out to R. Brett & Sons for a time. Some time later she was sold to Hillhead Quarries Ltd of Buxton, Derbyshire. This photograph was taken after an accident in which she finished up hitting the George Hotel in Buxton. The wagon was badly damaged and was sold for scrap to William Twigg of Matlock, Derbyshire, *circa* 1935. *(courtesy late T.B. Paisley)*

85.   Foden 'E' class six wheel undertype wagon No 13356, Registration No KP 8501, was built in July 1929 and sold to Marley Tile Co Ltd, of Harrietsham in Kent. She became No 8 in their fleet and spent the whole of her working life working from the Leighton Buzzard factory in Bedfordshire. In this photograph she is seen at Foden's works prior to delivery.   *(author's collection)*

86.   Foden 'N' class undertype wagon No 13400, Registration No LG 9336, was built in 1929 as an experimental model and was the only one of her type. She was made up of 'E' type components built into a chassis of new design fitted with an enclosed cab and running on pneumatic tyres. After approximately three years of development testing she was sold to F. Hackney of Elworth, Cheshire, but by January 1934 she had been acquired by William Thomas of Chester where she was last licenced in October 1934 after which she was scrapped.

(author's collection)

87.

88.   Foden 'E' class undertype wagon No 13446, Registration No UY 6444, was built in September 1929 and sold to William Holmes of Rubery, Worcestershire. In 1931 she was purchased by W.T. & A. Jackson of Fernhead in Lancashire. On this pre-delivery photograph, Fodens had the background painted out for use in one of their catalogues.   *(author's collection)*

89.   Foden 12 ton overtype six-wheeled tipping wagon No 13622, Registration No RB 2985, was built in November 1930 and sold to John Greenwood of Glossop, Derbyshire. Later, the date is not recorded, she was acquired by the Gypsum Company of Ireland, of Carrickmacross, Co Monaghan, her last recorded owner.

(author's collection)

90.   Foden S6 six ton undertype wagon No 13678, Registration No KR 7590, was built in November 1930 and sold to Martin & Sillett of Strood, Kent. In this photograph, taken at the time of delivery, she is seen fitted with the troublesome No 1 type boiler. A year after being delivered she received a No 2 type boiler but for how many years she worked after this is not recorded.   *(author's collection)*

91.   Foden S6 six ton undertype wagon No 13690, Registration No RB 1547, was built in May 1930 and sold to Road Products Ltd of Buxton, Derbyshire. She suffered boiler problems like so many 'S' types requiring a new No 2 type boiler in November after only six months work. This photograph shows her fitted with tar spraying equipment, a popular use for steam wagons as the readily available steam was an easy way of providing the heat to melt the tar.   *(author's collection)*

92. Foster 5 ton overtype wagon No 14483, Registration No AW 9392, was built in February 1921 and sold to Burd & Davies of Shrewsbury, her only recorded owner. Her driver proudly poses for the photographer
(courtesy J.L. Middlemiss)

93. Driver Tom Glover leans on the mudguard of a Foster 5 ton overtype wagon in use as a demonstrator on trade plates. Regretfully it is not possible to identify the number of the wagon.
(author's collection)

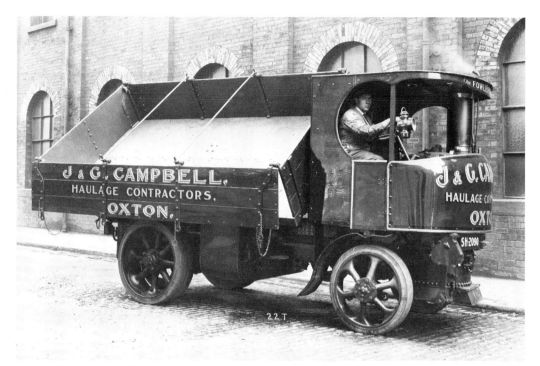

94. Fowler 6/7 ton undertype wagon fitted with 3-way tipping body No 16467, Registration No SH 2090, was built in May 1925 and sold to J. & G Campbell of Oxton, Berwick. She was last licenced in December 1927 being returned to Fowlers works in the same month where she was later scrapped. *(author's collection)*

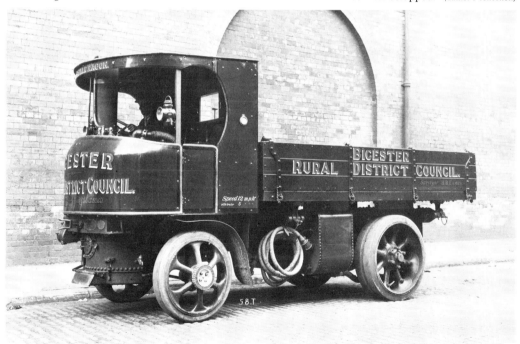

95. Fowler 6/7 ton undertype wagon fitted with 3-way tipping body No 16498 was built in 1925 and sent to Buenos Aires on a demonstration tour. After returning to England she was exhibited at the Royal Show at Reading in 1926 possibly after she had been sold to Bicester Urban District Council in June when she received the Registration No UD 218. *(author's collection)*

96.   Garrett 5 ton overtype wagon No 32442, Registration No BJ 2216, was built in August 1914 for the Moorhey Carrying Company of Oldham, Lancashire, where she became their fleet No 7. By 1924 she had been sold to G.F. Wood for scrapping.   *(courtesy T. Varley)*

97.   Garrett 4 ton overtype wagon No 32882, Registration No BJ 3006, was built in May 1916 for Boots of Nottingham. She was sold in 1924 to Lynx Motors Ltd of Malvern Links, Worcestershire, where she was last licenced in 1927. This vehicle was fitted with the Garrett superheater which accounts for the unusual shape of the smokebox. Photograph was taken at Daybrook, Nottingham in 1921   *(courtesy F.H. Gillford)*

98. Garrett 3 ton overtype wagon No 32914, Registration No BJ 3194, was built in August 1916 and sold to the Shipley Carbonising Company of Shipley in the West Riding of Yorkshire. She was last licenced in 1927 but lingered on for six years before being sold for scrap to G.W. Butler of Otley, W.R. This photograph shows her after having skidded off the road, narrowly missing a telegraph pole but demolishing a stone wall.

(courtesy T.B. Paisley)

99. Garrett 3 ton overtype wagon No 32960, Registration No BJ 3264, was built in December 1916 and sold to E. Clover of Dedham, Essex, where she spent her working life. She had been scrapped by 1933.

(courtesy R.G. Pratt)

100. Garrett 5 ton overtype tipping wagon No 33100 was built in July 1917 for the Ministry of Munitions. By 1923 she had been sold to James Stuart & Son of Kirriemuir, Angus. The registration number she should have received at this time is not recorded. This nearside view clearly illustrates the belt attached to the flywheel which drove the body tipping mechanism. *(courtesy J.L. Middlemiss)*

101. Garrett 5 ton overtype tipping wagon No 33194 was built in November 1917 for the Ministry of Munitions. In 1919 she was sold to the Devonshire County Council (Northern Division) receiving the Registration No T 6838 and spent the rest of her working life with this authority being last licenced in 1950. *(courtesy W.A. Briggs)*

102.   Garrett 4 ton overtype wagon No 34415, Registration No BJ 8955, was built in January 1924 and sold to D. Quinton & Sons of Needham Market, East Suffolk. In October 1935 she was sold to C.J. Hales of Beccles for scrap.   *(courtesy R.G. Pratt)*

103.   Garrett 5 ton overtype tipping wagon No 34443, Registration No PW 2186, was built in February 1924 and sold to Burrell's Hiring Company of Thetford. This was presumably on a five year contract as in 1929 she became the property of Edward J. Edwards of Norwich. This photograph was taken in Orwell Road, Ipswich in May 1933.   *(courtesy R.G. Pratt)*

104.   Garrett 6 ton undertype wagon No 35331, Registration No KR 783, was built in November 1929 and sold to Herbert & Blunt of Sholden, Deal, in Kent. This photograph was taken at the works just prior to delivery.   *(courtesy B.D. Stoyel)*

105.   Garrett 10 ton undertype tipping wagon No 35372, Registration No DV 4599, was built in March 1930 and sold to William Elworthy of Tiverton, Devon. By 1932 she had been sold to Lynx Motors Ltd of Malvern Link, Worcestershire, possibly as a result of the accident seen in this illustration which took place at Budleigh Salterton railway bridge in the summer of 1931. She was last licenced in November 1933.

(courtesy B.D.Stoyel)

106. A pre-delivery photograph of Garrett 8 ton undertype tipping wagon No 35456, Registration No KR 9788, which was built in March 1931 and sold to Harber Bros of Swanley, Kent. *(courtesy B.D. Stoyel)*

107. Garrett 8 ton undertype wagon No 35460, Registration No UP 5562, was built in May 1931 and sold to Robert B. Parker of Leadgate, Co Durham. In March 1932 she was sold to J.W. & A. Pearl of Otley, East Suffolk, later being sold to William J. Rush of Tannington where she was last licenced in December 1936.

(courtesy R.G. Pratt)

108. Glasgow 5 ton undertype lorry No 3, Registration No V 416, was built in 1906 for the Motor Transit Company Ltd of Leith, Scotland. In July 1907 the company changed its name from the Glasgow Motor Lorry Co Ltd to Halley's Industrial Motors Ltd and from this time on their efforts seemed to favour the petrol vehicle and steam took second place.   *(courtesy J.L. Thomas)*

109. This Hora 4 ton undertype wagon was built by August 1906 and sold to R. White & Sons Ltd, of Camberwell, London. E. & M. Hora Ltd, of Peckham, London only produced one, or possibly two, wagons and very little is known about the company or the mechanical specifications of its vehicles.

(courtesy B.D. Stoyel)

110 & 111. Lancashire
'B' class 4 ton undertype
wagon built between the years
1901 and 1904. This design of
vehicle was the first to be built
in quantity by the Lancashire
Steam Motor Company and was
eventually superceded by the
'H' class in 1904. The version
illustrated was modified for
colonial use with perch bracket
steering.

In 1907 the company changed
its name to the Leyland Motor
Company Ltd, a name that has
stayed with us until recent
times.

*(courtesy the British Commercial
Vehicle Museum)*

112.   A Lancashire 5 ton 'H' class undertype tipping wagon built in 1906, Registration number probably B 2052 (B2K was a firm's trade plate), and sold to White Star Line Works of Bootle, Lancashire, where she became No 1 in their fleet. She was later acquired by Harland & Wolff Ltd of Bootle and was last licenced in 1937.
(courtesy The British Commercial Vehicle Museum)

113.   Leyland 'H class undertype tipping wagon with dustcart body, Registration No LG 7749, built in 1907 and sold to Chelsea Corporation where she became their fleet No 9.
(courtesy T.B. Paisley)

114 & 115. Leyland 'H' class undertype wagon, Registration No B 2137, was built *circa* 1907 and sold to the Barnet District Gas & Water Company. She was last licenced in 1922. *(Above)* The crew pose in front of the wagon at the gas works; and *(below)* dressed with flowers and complete with band she takes part in a carnival parade, *circa* 1919, to raise money for the local hospital.

(author's collection)

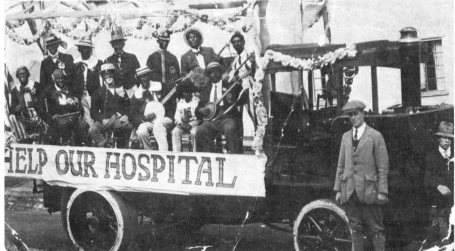

116. Leyland 'H' class undertype wagon No H126 588 was built *circa 1909*and was also sold to the Barnet District Gas & Water Company, where she became their fleet No 3. The photograph shows her at Barnet Gasworks prior to taking part in a trade procession, *circa* 1920.

(author's collection)

117.   Leyland 'F' class undertype wagon, Registration No B 5700, was built *circa 1913* and sold to H. Viney & Co Ltd of Preston, Lancashire, where she became No 27 in their fleet. At some period during her working life she was converted to a tractor unit for use with a semi-trailer as shown in this photograph. She spent all of her time with this company and was last licenced in 1931.   *(courtesy The British Commercial Vehicle Museum)*

118.   Leyland Class 'F' undertype wagon, Registration No CK 457, was built in May 1912 and sold to H. Viney & Co Ltd of Preston, Lancashire, where she became their fleet No 12. She had been scrapped by February 1933.   *(courtesy B.D. Stoyel)*

119.   Leyland 6 ton 'F' class undertype wagon No F2-22-1581, Registration No TB 1152, was built between the years 1911 and 1920 and sold to Henry Tate & Sons Ltd (later Tate & Lyle) of Liverpool. She spent her entire working life with this company and was last licenced in 1947.

(courtesy The British Commercial Vehicle Museum)

120.   Leyland 'F2' class undertype tipping wagon No F2-2, Registration No B 8652, was built in July 1919 and sold to Lancashire County Council where she became No 4 in their fleet. She was later sold to Houghton & Robinson of Morecambe, Lancashire and was last licenced in 1933.

(courtesy The British Commercial Vehicle Museum)

121.   Leyland 6 ton 'F2' class undertype wagon No F2/35-1692, Registration No TB 1428, was built *circa* 1921 and sold to McFie & Sons Ltd of Liverpool, where she became No 8 in their fleet. She spent her working life with this company and was last licenced in January 1932.   *(courtesy The British Commercial Vehicle Museum)*

122.   Leyland undertype tipping wagon No F2-110, Registration No TB 678, built in August 1921 and sold to Garstang Rural District Council where she became No 1 in their fleet. In 1930 she was burnt out but was rebuilt and re-registered in 1931 becoming CK 4581 and number 10 in the Lancashire County Council fleet. She was sold in 1934 and scrapped.   *(courtesy The British Commercial Vehicle Museum)*

123. Leyland 'F2' class undertype wagon No F2/90, Registration No XD 8298. Built in June 1921 and sold equipped as a gully emptier to Islington Borough Council, in London. In August 1929 she was sold for scrap to T.W. Ward Ltd. *(courtesy British Commercial Vehicle Museum)*

124. The remains of Leyland 'F' class undertype wagon, Registration No TC 1715, which was built in November 1922 and sold to J. Whittaker & Son Ltd of Edenfield, near Ramsbottom, Lancashire. This photograph was taken at Scout Moor Quarries, Edenfield on 17th May 1947. *(W.P. Riley, courtesy B.D. Stoyel)*

125. Londonderry 5 ton undertype wagon No 21, Registration No AC 485, was built in October 1904 and sold to the Jones Haulage Syndicate of Hampton-in-Arden, Warwickshire.
(courtesy B.D. Stoyel)

126. Londonderry 5 ton undertype wagon, Registration No IJ 87, was built in 1904 and sold to the Belfast & County Down Railway of Northern Ireland.
(courtesy B.D. Stoyel)

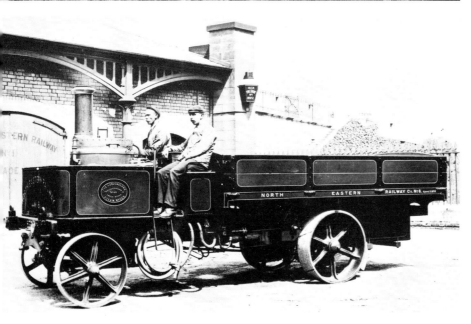

127. Londonderry 5 ton undertype wagon No 38, Registration No BT 204, was built in July 1905 and sold to the North Eastern Railway Company. Built by the Seaham Harbour Engine Works of Durham and named after the firm's proprietor the Marquis of Londonderry.
(courtesy North Yorkshire Moors Railway Preservation Society)

128.   Manns 5 ton undertype steam cart of the 1903 design, Registration No C 707, built *circa* 1903/5 and seen in this photograph transporting bricks from Ripon Station to Carlesmoor Tunnel.   *(courtesy T. Varley)*

129.   Manns 5 ton undertype wagon, Registration No C 520, was built in 1904 and sold to Bentley's Yorkshire Breweries Ltd, of Woodlesford, West Riding, where she became No 2 in their fleet. This photograph clearly shows the additional steering wheel on the left side of the vehicle which was available as an optional extra. Although designed for one man operaton it enabled the assistant to steer while the driver looked after his fire which was only accessible from his side of the cab. It was also a good way of initiating the assistant into the handling of the wagon.   *(courtesy D.A. Rayner)*

130.   Manns 3 ton undertype wagon No 200, Registration No U 764 was built in 1905 and sold to R. Jones of Penmachno, Caernarvon. By July 1922 she had been sold to John Roberts & Sons of Llantwst, Denbigh who last licensed her in June 1924. Photograph shows the wagon about to begin a coal delivery with R. Jones, the owner, driving.   *(courtesy J.W. Cole)*

131.   Manns 5 ton undertype wagon on test loaded with one ton weights, *circa* 1905. The Registration No UM 18 is probably a trade plate used by the makers for testing and delivery purposes.   *(author's collection)*

132.   Manns 5 ton undertype wagon built in 1905 and sold to the Midland Railway Company for use at their goods depot at Bath where she became their fleet No 6974. The Registration No UM33 is probably the maker's trade plate number used for delivery of new wagons and for demonstration purposes. Three of these wagons were sold to the Midland Railway Company at Bath, ultimately receiving the Registration Nos FB 015, FB 016 and FB 017.   *(author's collection)*

133.   Manns 5 ton undertype wagon No 343, Registration No U 353, built in September 1906 and sold to Barnby Bendall & Co of Cheltenham. By February 1921 she had been sold to Thomas A. Howells of Hereford who resold her the same month to John Reahorn of Brynmawr, Brecon who scrapped her *circa* 1923.

(courtesy D.C. Bendall)

134.   Manns 3 ton undertype wagon, Registration No F 2106, was built *circa* 1906 and sold to Albert E. Farr of Frinton on Sea, Essex. In 1911 she was sold to Arthur Hutley of Coggeshall, Essex.   *(courtesy D.A. Rayner)*

135.   Mann's 5 ton undertype tipping wagon No 535, Registration No U 1107, was built in 1908 and sold to John Thomas of Toncwynlais, near Cardiff. This photograph was taken on the 9th August 1908 at the time of delivery. Manns delivery driver, W. Wintringham, 'Scarborough Billy', is in the driver's seat, whilst the owner's son stands to the rear of the wagon and his grandson at the front.   *(courtesy J.W. Cole)*

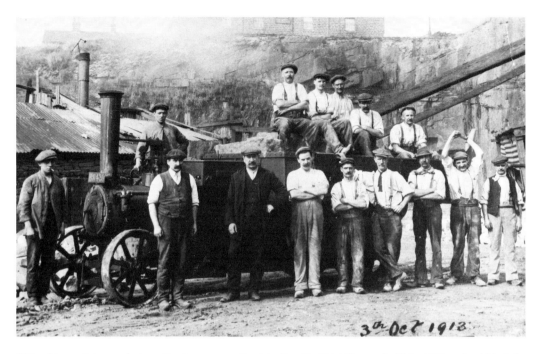

136.   Manns 5 ton undertype tipping wagon, Registration No BN 436, was built in 1908 and sold to John Best & Sons of Edinburgh. This photograph taken on the 3rd October 1913 shows her at work at the Delph Reservoir in the West Riding of Yorkshire.   *(courtesy B.D. Stoyel)*

137.   Manns 5 ton overtype steam cart, possibly works number 914, Registration No U 2573, built in March 1914 and sold to Sir Charles Seely, bart, of Arnold Nottinghamshire, photographed at Daybrook, Nottinghamshire in 1916.   *(courtesy F.H. Gillford)*

138. Manns 3 ton tipping wagon No 944, Registration No F 9670, was built in December 1914 and sold to Walthamstow Urban District Council, in Essex, where she became their fleet No 4. In 1926 she was sold to Joseph Coles & Sons of West Town, Somerset and was finally scrapped in 1928. *(courtesy T.B. Paisley)*

139. Mann's 3 ton overtype wagon No 1078, Registration No U 3287, was built in June 1915 and sold to Morris & Co (Ampthill), Bedfordshire. This brewery was taken over by J.W. Green Ltd of Luton in 1926. In 1927 they sold her to Thomas Oakley of Luton who was presumably a dealer as she was sold the same year to Thomas T. Boughton of Amersham Common, Buckinghamshire. This photograph was taken when the wagon was new and shows her about to set off on a delivery round driven by Monty Humberstone.

(courtesy Bedford Model Engineering Society)

140.   Manns overtype tipping wagon No 1337, Registration No U 4684, was built *circa* 1918 and sold to the Lancaster Corporation Gas Department where she spent her working life being licenced for the last time in December 1935. This wagon was one of a special narrow track design.   *(W.P. Riley, courtesy B.D. Stoyel)*

141.   Pictured taking a rest after loading his wagon with coal is the driver of Manns 3 ton overtype tipping wagon No 1369, Registration No U 4868, was built *circa* 1919. Her first owner is not recorded but by January 1927 she had been sold to James Critchley & Sons Ltd, of Batley in the West Riding of Yorkshire who last licenced her in March 1933.   *(courtesy Mrs J. Hampshire)*

142. Manns 5 ton overtype tipping wagon No 1479, Registration No U 5933, was built in 1920 and sold to the Lancaster Corporation where she became No 2 in their fleet. She was last licenced in December 1935.

(W.P. Riley, courtesy B.D. Stoyel)

143. Manns 5 ton overtype wagon No 1565, Registration No WY 3810, was built in May 1922 and sold to G. Armitage & Sons Ltd of Robin Hood, West Riding of Yorkshire. In 1928 she was sold to P.W. Spencer of Giggleswick, also in the West Riding. Illustrated carting bricks whilst in the ownership of G. Armitage & Sons Ltd.

(courtesy J.W. Cole)

144.   An unidentified Manns 5 ton undertype wagon, possibly belonging to Webber & Stedham of Torquay, in trouble at Torquay having run over the edge of the harbour wall.   *(courtesy J.W. Cole)*

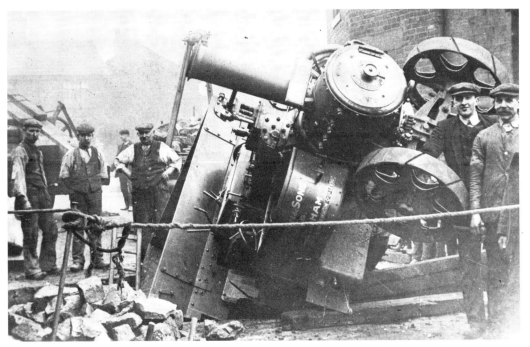

145.   Mann 5 ton overtype tipping cart, Registration No U 1160, in trouble having fallen through the road into a sewer in Main Street, Hollinwood, near Oldham, Lancashire. The man holding the hammer to the right of the picture is W. Wintringham, known as 'Scarborough Billy', one of Manns' delivery drivers. The works number of the engine and the date of this accident regretfully are not recorded.   *(courtesy J.W. Cole)*

146. Manns 'Express' 6 ton undertype tipping wagon sold to M. Furness & Sons of Eyam, West Riding of Yorkshire. The 'Express' range of vehicles were introduced in 1924 and although of a very advanced design it would appear that not many more than twelve were built as it was not put into full scale production.

(courtesy T.B. Paisley)

147. Manns overtype wagon No 1639, Registration No NK 7650, was built in April 1924, and sold to McMullen & Sons Ltd of Hertford. After ten years of work she was sold in 1934 to scrap dealer George Taylor of Redbourn, Hertfordshire where she is pictured laying derelict on 22nd June 1936.

(courtesy R.G. Pratt)

148. A Manns 6 ton overtype wagon standing derelict in the yard of George Hattersley & Son Ltd of Keighley, in the West Riding of Yorkshire on 24th September 1951. She is possibly No 1722, Registration No WU 5251, built in March 1926 and sold to the above firm.

(W.P. Riley, courtesy B.D. Stoyel)

149. Nayler undertype wagon, Registration No CJ 67, built in 1903. By March 1904 she had been sold to Henry Whitmore Ltd of Romford, Essex. In 1910 she went to E. Layzell of Southend on Sea, in 1913 to Arthur R. Crouch of Southchurch, Essex and finally, in 1915, to her last recorded owner, J.H.G.M. MacMatton.
(courtesy R. Smith)

150. A Nayler undertype wagon and trailer, an interesting feature of which, though not clearly discernible in this photograph, is the square section steering wheel. Regretfully there is no means of identifying the owner of this particular wagon.
(courtesy R. Smith)

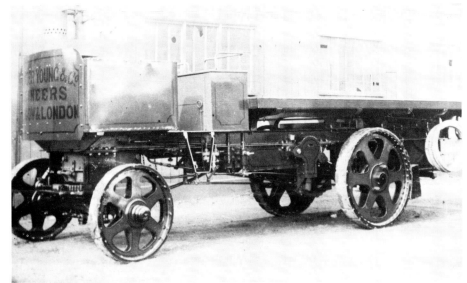

151. A Nayler undertype wagon belonging to Young & Company of Glasgow and London. This vehicle differs from the other two Naylers featured in having steel plate wheels.
(courtesy R. Smith)

152. A Ransomes, Sims & Jefferies overtype 3-way tipping wagon fitted with hydraulic tipping gear, photographed in the paint shop at Orwell Works, Ipswich. Unfortunately the number of the wagon is not recorded.
(author's collection)

153. Ransomes, Sims & Jefferies overtype wagon No 32152, Registration No DX3424, was built in January 1922, fitted with the Ransomes two wheel conversion attachment and used as a demonstrator. In the same year she was exhibited on the company's stand at the Royal Agricultural Society of England Annual Show which was held that year at Cambridge.
In February 1926 she was sold to W.J. Fisher, for the Rhodesia Chrome Mines Ltd at Selukwe, Rhodesia.
(courtesy Ransomes, Sims & Jefferies Ltd)

154. A Ridealgh 4 ton undertype wagon built *circa* 1920 at the engineering works of Thomas J. Ridealgh, Bradford, who was one time works manager at Manns. This vehicle was built up using the boiler and 4 cylinder poppet valve 'V' type engine that was used in the Summerscales tractor and was put to work hauling coal to the Bradford mills. Thomas Ridealgh later gave up his business and went to work for the Yorkshire Patent Steam Wagon Company at Leeds where he was responsible for the 'WG' series of wagons.
(courtesy J.W. Cole)

155. Robey's prototype steam wagon was this 5 ton undertype, No 25734, built in June 1906 and exhibited at the Royal Agricultural Society of England Annual Show at Derby in the same year. She spent her life on hire and loan for evaluation and demonstration purposes; on 12th September to the Great Central Railway Company, 11th to 15th October to the Motor Delivery Company Ltd of London, on 1st November to Fisher & Company of Tamworth. In January 1907 she received the Registration No FE 298 and on the 10th of the month went to J. Glover Ltd, of Killamarsh, Derby. In April she was returned to the works and on 2nd May went to the Union Transit Company of Glasgow being returned to Robeys in June. Thereafter her wanderings are not recorded so she was possibly retired and broken up. *(courtesy D.A. Rayner)*

156. Robey 5 ton overtype wagon No 38501 was built in May 1919 and exhibited at the Royal Agricultural Society of England Show at Cardiff. On 7th June 1919 she was sold to H. Newsum Sons & Co of Sheffield, when she received the Registration No FE 2726. Her last recorded owner was W. Malthouses Ltd, of Sheffield. *(courtesy D.A. Rayner)*

157. Robey 5 ton overtype
wagon No 38502, Registration
No FE 2725, was built in
August 1919 and sold to W.J.
Pullen Ltd of Sittingbourne,
Kent. In 1920 she went to West
Kent Works Ltd, at Westerham,
Kent and finished up with
H.W. Clarke of Erith, Kent.
(courtesy B.D. Stoyel)

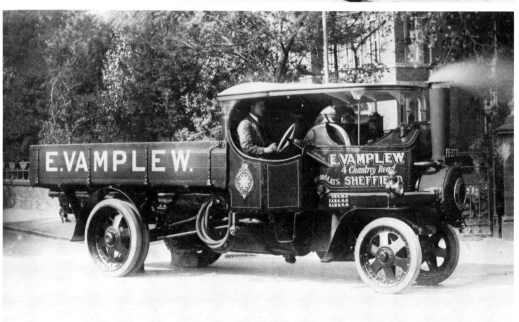

158. Robey 5 ton overtype wagon No 38503, Registration No FE 2771 was built in September 1919 and sold to Mrs Esther Vamplew of Woodseats, Sheffield. In January 1925 she was returned to the works and Robeys sold her in July to Gould Bros of Hillsborough, Sheffield, later going to John Wood & Son of Sheffield, her last recorded owner.

(courtesy D.A. Rayner)

159.   Robey 5 ton overtype wagon No 38511, Registration No FE 3041, was built in January 1920 and sold to John Laing & Son of Carlisle. She was later sold to the Allweather Mechanical Grouting Company Ltd.

(courtesy R. Hooley)

160.   Robey 5 ton overtype tipping wagon No 38512, Registration No FE 3042, was built in January 1920 and sold to Whiteway & Ball Ltd of Torquay, Devon. In 1933 she was sold to the Mechanical Hot & Cold Tar Spraying Company Ltd of Newton Abbot, Devon.

(courtesy R. Hooley)

161. Robey 5 ton overtype wagon No 40682, Registration No WA 9866, was built in March 1924 and sold to I. Vamplew & Sons of Woodseats, Sheffield. By December 1926 she had been returned to Robeys who then sold her, in April 1930, to Swift Bros of Renishaw, Sheffield. Her last owner was Allweather Mechanical Grouting Co Ltd of London SW1 who bought her in 1931 and last licenced her in December 1945.
(courtesy B.D. Stoyel)

162. A Robey 6 ton overtype wagon, (probably No 42288) seen in the workshops of the British Ceylon Corporation undergoing major repairs in 1972.
(courtesy F. Jones)

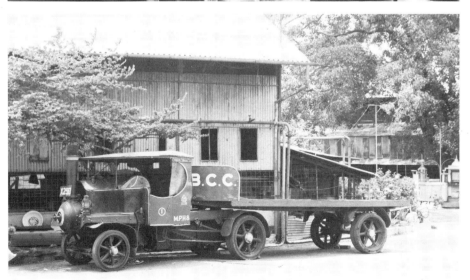

163. A photograph taken at Colombo, Ceylon, in 1972 of Robey 10 ton overtype articulated wagon No 43757, built in 1928 and sold to the British Ceylon Corporation where she became No 1 in their fleet. Her Ceylon Registration No was X 2553.
(courtesy F. Jones)

164 & 165. Two Robey works photographs. The upper illustration shows a Robey wagon and trailer in a typical street scene. The lower one is the same photograph adapted for advertising purposes directed at the fish trade. The background has been painted out and the artist has obligingly added the boxes of fish and has lettered the wagon and trailer to suit the advertisement.

(courtesy R. Hooley)

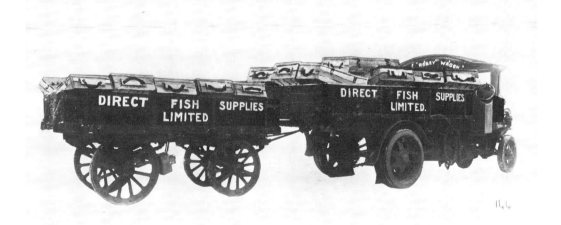

166.   The prototype St Pancras 5 ton undertype wagon, Registration No A 7311, built in 1904 , posed in the doorway of Chubb's works in Glengall Road, North London. The footscraper in the wall of the building must have been appreciated judging by the condition of the road.   *(courtesy Chubb archives)*

167.   Another picture of the first St Pancras wagon. Mr T.P Chubb was the secretary of the St Pancras Ironworks Company, so it was natural that the first vehicle was used by Chubb's for delivering their safes.

(courtesy Chubb Archives)

168.   Another interesting picture of the first St Pancras wagon, taken on the 7th December 1904 together
with the previous two views, outside Chubb's North London works.   *(courtesy Chubb Archives)*

169.   St Pancras 5 ton undertype wagon, Registration No BT 203 at York (see No. 170)
(courtesy North Yorkshire Moors Railway Preservation Society)

170. Another interesting view of St Pancras 5 ton undertype wagon, Registration No BT 203, built in July 1905 and sold to the North Eastern Railway Company where she became their fleet No 7. This vehicle is fitted with their improved watertube boiler. Photographs taken at York at the time of delivery.

(courtesy North Yorkshire Moors Railway Preservation Society)

171. St Pancras 5 ton undertype wagon, Registration No L 3599, was built in January 1906 and sold to J.W. Lance of Lymington, Hants. Writing of the vehicle, which appeared to be giving him great satisfaction he said, 'The work done is general cartage and furniture removal, and it has climbed the High Street in this town with a load of over four tons, the hill being 1 in 7 at the top. (courtesy G. Hedges)

172.   The St Pancras wagon of Mr J.W. Lance loaded with 4 tons of coke about to leave Poole Gasworks bound for Wimbourne Waterworks, a distance of seven miles which it achieved twice a day for a number of weeks.)
(courtesy G. Hedges)

173.   Savage class 'OA' undertype tipping wagon built in 1905 and sold to the Corporation of Leicester Highways & Sewerage Department.
(courtesy J.L. Middlemiss)

174. A Savage undertype wagon photographed in the works yard at Kings Lynn, Norfolk sometime between 1904 and 1908. Unfortunately it is not possible to identify the vehicle so no further details are known.
(courtesy J.L. Middlemiss)

175. Sentinel 6 ton Standard undertype waggon, possibly No 102, Registration No V 344, was built in 1906 and was one of the first six production waggons built by Alley & MacLellan of Polmadie, Glasgow. She was sold to Cranes Motor Express of Airdrie, Lanarkshire. In 1915 the makers moved south to Shrewsbury and in 1917 changed their name to Sentinel Waggon Works Ltd.
(courtesy B.D. Stoyel)

176.   Sentinel 6 ton Standard undertype waggon No 129, Registration No V 435, was built in 1907 and sold to James Dewe, of Burghfield, Reading. She was later acquired by Clarks Ltd, also of Burghfield.

(courtesy B.D.Stoyel)

177.   Sentinel 3 ton Standard undertype waggon No 1329, Registration No AW 3048, was built *circa* 1916 and sold to Dan Lewis of Hanley, Stoke-on-Trent. She was later sold to E.B. Ward of Stockton Heath, Cheshire before going to her last owner, Richard Allen of Widnes, Lancashire.   *(courtesy B.D. Stoyel)*

178.   An unusual use for a Standard Sentinel waggon, the number of which is not recorded. During the latter stages of the First World War aircraft were beginning to operate at a height which necessitated the use of oxygen by the crews and this photograph shows one of the mobile oxygen producing plants which the RAF had to meet this need. The waggon is fitted with a Peter Brotherhood compressor driven by a 100hp Ricardo petrol engine and the chassis is supported on jacks to prevent excessive vibration.   *(author's collection)*

179.   Sentinel Standard undertype waggon No 2022, Registration No AW 4206, was built in July 1918 and sold to Stone & Co Ltd of Leicester, where she became No 2 in their fleet. She worked for this owner all her life and was last licenced in March 1926. By October 1929 she had been scrapped.   *(courtesy B.D. Stoyel)*

180.   Sentinel 6 ton Standard undertype waggon No 2973 ■, Registration No AW 6682, was built in 1920 and sold to Tennant Brothers Ltd of Sheffield. She was later sold to Brown Bayley's Steel Works Ltd, also of Sheffield, where she became No 3 in their fleet. She worked for this company until sold for preservation in the sixties. Photographed on test just prior to delivery.   *(courtesy B.D. Stoyel)*

181.   A Sentinel 6 ton Standard undertype waggon, probably No 3728, Registration No AW 8811, built *circa* 1920 and sold to N. Kilvert & Son of Trafford Park, Manchester, where she became No 14 in their fleet.

(courtesy B.D. Stoyel)

182. Super Sentinel 6 ton undertype waggon No 5210, Registration No WT 1607, was built in 1924. The first eight years of her life are not recorded but by 1932 she was with the Holt Lane Stone Co Ltd, of Prescot, Lancashire.) *(courtesy C. Roades)*

183. Super Sentinel undertype waggon No 6400, Registration No BA 5665, was built in February 1926 and sold to Topham Bros (Manchester) Ltd, where she was fleet No 17. In 1937 she was sold to W.J. Glossop Ltd, of Hipperholme in the West Riding of Yorkshire, receiving their fleet No 120.
(courtesy F. Jones)

184. Super Sentinel undertype waggon No 6606, Registration No YU 771, was built in October 1927 and sold to Gardiner & Tidy (Farrands Cherry Garden Wharf) of Bermondsey, London, where she became their fleet No 4. In 1936 she was sold to H.V. Smith & Co Ltd of Tottenham, Middlesex and was still in their ownership when this photograph was taken in 1953.

(courtesy F. Jones)

185. Sentinel DG6 undertype waggon No 7537, Registration No CF 8662, was built in August 1928 and sold to H.H. Kemp & Son of Sudbury, Suffolk. Later in her life she was sold to Speechley's Ltd, of Alperton, Middlesex.

(courtesy R.G. Pratt)

186. Sentinel DG6 undertype waggon No 7709, Registration No TM 4214, was built in February 1929 and sold to H.G. Brown & Son of Leighton Buzzard, Bedfordshire, where she was No 20 in their fleet. This photograph was taken at Shrewsbury in 1929 and shows Harry Brown collecting the wagon from the works.

(courtesy P. Brown)

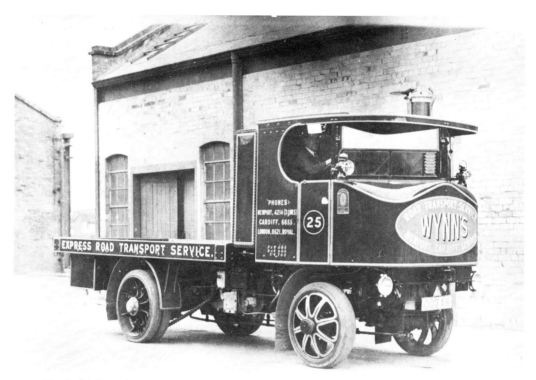

187. Sentinel DG4 undertype waggon No 7746, Registration No DW 6440, was built in 1929 and sold to Robert Wynn & Co Ltd of Newport, Monmouthshire, where she became No 25 in their fleet.

(courtesy B.D. Stoyel)

188. Sentinel DG6 undertype waggon No 7953, Registration No KP 8414. Built in July 1929 and sold to Thomas Wood & Sons Ltd, of Crockenhill, Kent, where she became No 11 in their fleet.

(courtesy Thomas Wood & Sons Ltd)

189. Sentinel DG4 undertype waggon No 8388, Registration No KF 2205, was built in August 1930 and sold to L.F. Briggs Ltd, of Liverpool, where she became their fleet No 28. The wagon just behind is No 8387, Registration No KF 2206, fleet No 29. They remained with L.F. Briggs Ltd for all their working lives and were both licenced for the last time in December 1934. *(courtesy B.D. Stoyel)*

190. Sentinel DG8 undertype 3-way tipping waggon No 8420 was built in January 1931 and sold to George Phillipson & Sons of Cox Green, Bolton, Lancashire, where she became their fleet No 3. *(courtesy B.D. Stoyel)*

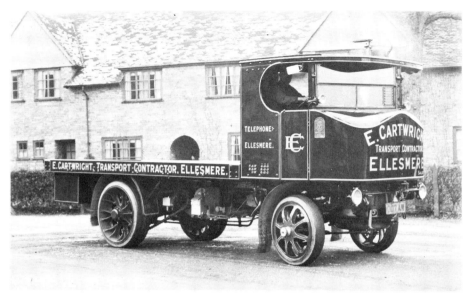

191. Sentinel DG4 undertype waggon No 8453, Registration No UX 8110, was built in January 1931 and sold to E. Cartwright of Ellesmere Port, Cheshire. In August 1932 she was sold to Rupert Pedley of Wooburn Green, going to Jas. Osbourne of Kilmarnock in March 1934. Later she finished up with A. & J. McLellan Ltd of Glasgow.

(author's collection)

192. Sentinel DG4 undertype tipping waggon No 8575, Registration No OU 9426, was built in September 1931 and supplied to Hampshire County Council, her only recorded owner.

(courtesy B.D. Stoyel)

193. Sentinel DG4 undertype waggon No 8704, Registration No XJ 1773, was built in November 1932 and sold to H.A. Newport of Fordham, Cambridgeshire, where she became No 32 in their fleet.

(courtesy R.G. Prat

194. Sentinel S6 undertype waggon No 8849, Registration No GL 838, was built in August 1933 and sold to the City Steam Transport Company of Bath, their fleet No 18. She was later sold to T.T. Boughton & Sons of Amersham Common, Buckinghamshire and they scrapped her in 1952. *(courtesy Thomas Wood & Sons Ltd)*

195. Sentinel S4 undertype waggon No 8850 ■, Registration No FJ 9248, was built in October 1933 and sold to the Devon Trading Co Ltd, of Bideford, North Devon. She was later acquired by the Teignmouth Quay Co Ltd of Teignmouth, South Devon. This photograph was taken at Teignmouth Quay on 21st June 1961 and three years later she was sold into preservation. *(courtesy J.H. Meredith)*

196. Sentinel S4 undertype waggon No 8919, Registration No JG 4192, was built in January 1934 and sold to Kingsford & Co of Barton, Kent. She was later acquired by R.M. Woolley of Bucknell, Salop. When she was scrapped the boiler was transferred to the chassis of No 9346 which went to the USA in 1962. This photograph was taken at Paddock Wood, Kent in May 1948.

(courtesy W.S. Love)

197. Sentinel S4 undertype waggon No 9023 ■, Registration No AKR 958, was built in March 1934 and sold to H. Sargeant & Sons of Dover. She was later acquired by Wingham Engineering Company Ltd, Kent. In this photograph, taken on 13th April 1954, she is seen delivering beer in Dover whilst on hire to Fremlins, the brewers.

(courtesy J.J. Love)

198. Sentinel S4 undertype waggon No 9045, Registration No AYT 45, was built in June 1934 and sold to the South Metropolitan Gas Company of Greenwich, London where she became No 7 in their fleet. She was fitted with tar tank and spraying equipment. This photograph was taken when new at Shrewsbury.

(author's collection)

199. Sentinel S6 10 ton undertype waggon No 9084 ■, Registration No FH 8870, was built in April 1934 and sold to Priday & Metford & Company of Gloucester, where she became No 7 in their fleet. She was later sold to S. Llewellyn & Son of Ross, Herefordshire, followed by British Road Services and finally, in 1951, to R.M. Woolley of Bucknell, Salop, where she became No 10 in his fleet.

(courtesy F. Jones)

200. Sentinel S4 undertype waggon No 9227, Registration No CGW 845, was built in November 1935 and sold to the Gas Light & Coke Company, where she became No 845 in their fleet. She was later acquired by the North Thames Gas Board where she took No 267 in their fleet. This photograph was taken in Westminster Bridge Road on 9th November 1950.

(courtesy J.H. Meredith)

201. The first Sheppee wagon, Registration No DN 4, was built in August 1908 and sold in 1911 to Moore & Sharpe of Ovenden in the West Riding of Yorkshire. In 1914 she was purchased by Walter H. Welshman of Wolverhampton, finally going for scrap to Magill & Sons of Bilston. *(courtesy T. Varley)*

202. An unidentified Sheppee charabanc built *circa* 1913 and fitted with a let-down tail flap for light luggage. *(courtesy T. Varley)*

203. Sheppee 3 ton wagon, Registration No DN 9, was built in July 1913 and sold in 1915 to John Smith's Tadcaster Brewery Company Ltd. In 1919 she went to Leonard D. Chatt of Darlington only to be sold the following year to her last owner J. Ashton Riley Ltd of Huddersfield. *(courtesy T. Varley)*

204. Sheppee 3 ton wagon, Registration No DN 658, was built in September 1914 and later sold to Forster, Loverdale & Company Ltd, of York. In 1920 she was purchased by Joseph Davidson of Leeds and York.

(courtesy T. Varley)

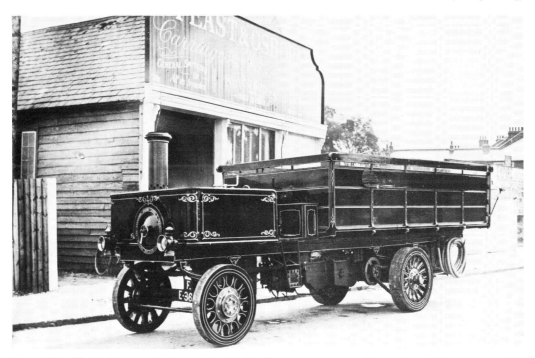

205. This official photograph of a 1907 Standard undertype wagon was taken on the 11th June 1907 outside the premises of body builders Messrs Feast & Osborne of Leigh on Sea, Essex. Towards the end of 1907 the firm changed it's name to T.J. Rayner & Sons but continued trading from Rayleigh in Essex. *(courtesy R.G. Pratt)*

206. Straker 5 ton undertype wagon, Registration No BB 88, was built *circa* 1902 and sold to Bainbridge & Company Ltd, of Newcastle-upon-Tyne.
(author's collection)

207. Straker 5 ton undertype wagon No 29 was built *circa* 1903 and sold to Woods, Sadd & Morse of Loddon, Norfolk.
(courtesy B.D. Stoyel)

208. Straker 5 ton undertype wagon, built *circa* 1903, Registration No L 103 and sold to W.J. Rogers Ltd of Bristol. About 1905 she was re-registered and given the number AE 696.

(courtesy B.D. Stoyel)

209. Straker 5 ton undertype wagon No 40, Registration No FB-10, was built in 1903 and sold to Stothert & Pitt Ltd of Bath.

(courtesy B.D. Stoyel)

210. A Straker 5 ton undertype wagon built in 1904 and supplied to the Admiralty for use at the Royal Naval Hospital at Chatham, Kent.

(courtesy B.D. Stoyel)

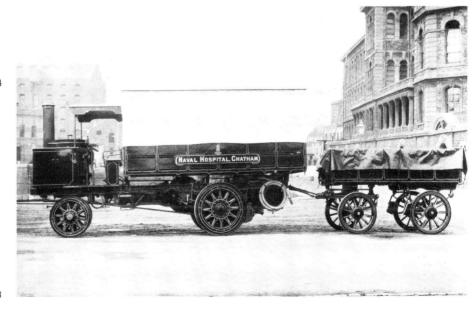

211.   Straker 5 ton undertype wagon No 101, Registration No BM 35, was built in 1904 and sold to George Horn of Kempston Mill, Bedfordshire. In 1912 she was sold to Herbert N. Harris of Bridport, Devon. The driver is William Morris with Mr William Horn standing at the rear of the vehicle.   *(courtesy J. Clover)*

212.   A Straker undertype wagon fitted with a bus body, Registration No E 192, built *circa* 1904 and sold to the North Staffordshire Railway Company. In 1906 she was sold to Arthur Wedgwood of Cobridge, Staffordshire, receiving the new Registration No EH-5. This photograph was taken at Ipstones railway station.   *(author's collection)*

213, 214 & 215.   Three interesting photographs of Straker undertype wagon No 120, Registration No CH 121, which was changed in August 1905 to FB-01. Built in April 1904 and sold to the Midland Railway Company for use at their Bath goods depot where she became No 5263 in the railway fleet. They last licenced her in February 1921. In the centre photograph she is seen in the Midland locomotive shed at Bath undergoing a major overhaul with the stripped down boiler in the foreground whilst the engine is receiving attention from a fitter. In the background can be seen part of a Johnson 4-4-0 passenger locomotive in un-rebuilt condition.

(author's collection)

216. Straker 5 ton undertype wagon No 129, was built in 1904 and sold to the North Eastern Railway Company for use at their Tollerton goods depot, where she was fleet No 1. *(courtesy North Yorkshire Moors Railway Preservation Society)*

217. Straker 5 ton overtype wagon No 204, Registration No LN 6645, was built in 1907 and entered in the RAC Trials.
(courtesy R.G. Pratt)

218. Tasker 5 ton overtype tipping wagon either NO 1849 or No 1850, was built in 1921 and supplied to Forfar County Council, Dundee District Committee. Two wagons were ordered and it is not possible from this side view to identify which of the two is illustrated. She was last licenced in either 1932 or 1933.
(courtesy B.D. Stoyel)

219 & 220. Tasker 5 ton overtype tipping wagon No 1912, Registration No TT 306, was built in June 1924 and sold to Fred Payne of Red Ball, Devon. She was later sold to Taylor Bros of Bildeston, West Suffolk where she was cut down to make into a tractor for timber hauling. She was last licenced in 1934 and in the lower illustration she is seen laying derelict in Taylor's yard.
(courtesy R.G. Pratt)

221. Thornycroft 3 ton undertype wagon No 14, was built in March 1899 and sold to Schweppes Ltd, of Hendon, Middlesex. In 1904 she received the Registration No H 1910.

(courtesy Cadbury Schweppes Ltd)

222. Thornycroft 3 ton undertype wagon No 18, Registration No D 533, was built in February 1900 and sold to Cannon & Gaze Ltd, of Erith, Kent. She was advertised for sale in February 1908.

(courtesy B.D. Stoyel)

223. Thornycroft undertype tipping wagon possibly No 60, was built in December 1901 and sold to the Birrim Valley Gold Mining & Dredging Company Ltd. In this photograph she is seen in the ownership of McEwen & Charter of Petone, New Zealand.

(W.P. Riley, courtesy B.D. Stoyel)

224.   Thornycroft undertype wagon, possibly No 105, Registration No OI-86, was built in February 1902 and sold to the Belfast & Northern Counties Railway Company. In July 1903 the company changed its name to the Midland Railway (Northern Counties Committee). If the wagon in this photograph is No 105 she also carried the Registration No IW-1, either before or after the picture was taken.   *(courtesy R.G. Pratt)*

225.   Thornycroft 6 ton undertype wagons Nos 165 and 163, Registration Nos H 317 and H 315, both built in February 1903 and sold to Watney Combe Reid & Company of London.   *(courtesy B.D. Stoyel)*

226, 227, 228, 229 & 230.
Thornycroft 4 ton undertype
wagon No 383, Registration No
CH 120, was built in October
1904 and sold to the Midland
Railway Company, where she
became fleet No 5264.
In 1905 she received the new
Registration No FE 159 and by
July 1917 she had been sold to
Charles G. Collis of Kettering,
Northants, her last recorded
owner.
The five views on this and the
opposite page show her going
about her work just after she
had been delivered to the
Midland goods depot at Bath.
(author's collection)

231. This photograph taken at Thornycrofts Basingstoke factory *circa* 1900 shows wagons under construction in the wheel and body shop.

(author's collection)

232. A Thornycroft 3 ton undertype wagon possibly giving a demonstration. The location is reputed to be at Bexley Mill.

(courtesy Bexley London Libraries)

233 & 234. Wallis & Steevens 5 ton overtype wagon No 2904, Registration No AA 2124, was built in June 1906 and sold to Miller Lilley of Honiton, Devon. She was noted as being for sale in June 1908 and by October 1911 had been sold to the Devon Trading Company Ltd. This vehicle was the prototype Wallis & Steevens wagon, production was to continue until 1925 by which time they had built a total of 127 vehicles.

(author's collection)

235 & 236.   Wallis & Steevens 5 ton overtype wagon No 2951 was built in May 1907 and sold to Ashbys Staines Brewery Ltd. In 1912 she was returned to Wallis & Steevens Ltd who then hired her out until selling her in 1913 to William Rawlings of Collingbourne Ducis, Wiltshire. She later went to Henry Lewis Senior of Reading and is noted as being advertised for sale in July 1918 and again during 1923. *(author's collection)*

237. Wallis & Steevens 5 ton overtype wagon No 7034 was built in June 1908 and hired out to W. & T. Robson Ltd, of London EC. In March 1909 she was sold to Smith & Company Lamberhurst Ltd, of Lamberhurst, Kent. She was noted as being advertised for sale in April 1914 and again in December 1915.

(author's collection)

238. Wallis & Steevens 5 ton overtype wagon No 7035, Registration No AA 2229, was built in April 1908 and sold to Pickfords Ltd, where she became No 60 in their fleet. By March 1921 she had been sold to Walter Webb & Company Ltd, of Southampton, her last recorded owner.

(author's collection)

239. Wallis & Steevens 5 ton overtype wagon No 7037, Registration No AA 2244, was built in May 1908 and sold to the exors of George Balls of Walthamstow, Essex. In 1909 she was sold to William Willett of London (Ealing and Hove), but by June 1918 she had gone to the Ministry of Food. *(author's collection)*

240. Wallis & Steevens 5 ton overtype tipping wagon No 7140 was built in May 1910 and sold to Giants Causeway Columnar Basalt Company Ltd of Portrush, Country Antrim. This wagon was the fourth tipping vehicle built out of a total of twenty-four. *(author's collection)*

241. Wallis & Steevens 5 ton overtype wagon No 7252, Registration No AA 2442, was built in August 1911 and sold to West Street Brewery Company Ltd, of Brighton, Sussex. In 1913 she was sold to Smithers & Sons Ltd, of Portslade, East Sussex and by June 1922 she was with John Alderman, of Par Harbour, Cornwall, her last recorded owner.   *(author's collection)*

242. Wallis & Steevens 5 ton overtype wagon No 7279 ■, Registration No AA 2470, was built in April 1912 and sold to Pickfords Ltd, where she became their fleet No 104. By October she had been sold to J.W. Lance & Son of Lymington, Hampshire and was destined to have four more owners before being sold derelict for preservation in 1963.   *(author's collection)*

243. Wallis & Steevens 5 ton overtype wagon No 7280, Registration No AA 5008, was built in June 1912 and sold to Ashby's Staines Brewery Ltd. In 1917 she was returned to Wallis & Steevens who sold her the same year to the Associated Coal Consumers Ltd, of Fulham, London. In 1922 she was sold to a customer in Derbyshire but no other details are known.   *(author's collection)*

244. Wallis & Steevens 3 ton overtype wagon No 7282 was built in February 1912 and sold to Pickfords Ltd, where she became No 98 in their fleet. By July 1919 she had been sold to J.S. Spring & Company of Godalming, Surrey. Later the same year she was returned to Wallis & Steevens Ltd.
(author's collection)

245. Wallis & Steevens 3 ton overtype wagon No 7579, Registration No HO 6082, was built in June 1922 and hired out to Staines Brewery Ltd. In November 1922 the Registration No was changed to HO 6142 and she was then hired out to Portals Ltd, of Laverstoke, Hampshire. In June 1925 she was sold to James Kelly of Limavady, County Derry but in 1927 ownership reverted to Wallis & Steevens Ltd. She was then sold to J.B. Warke & Co of Castlerock in the same year and is photographed in derelict condition in their yard in June 1947.
(courtesy R.G. Pratt)

118

246, 247 & 248. Wallis & Steevens works photographs of their 5 ton overtype 3-way tipping wagon No 7718, Registration No IW 4791. Built in June 1923 and sold to J.B. Warke & Company of Castlerock, County Derry, who still owned her in July 1948.

(author's collection)

249. Wantage undertype wagon, Registration No FC 41, was built in 1903 and sold to W.G. Phillips & Sons Ltd, of the Tower Brewery, Oxford. *(courtesy B.D. Stoyel)*

250. Wantage undertype wagon, Registration No FC 93, was built in 1903 and sold to Saunders & Company of Oxford. *(courtesy T.B. Paisley)*

251. Yorkshire 4 ton
undertype tipping wagon
No 44, Registration No P 930,
was built in February 1904 and
sold to Hall & Company Ltd, of
Croydon, Surrey. Photograph
taken shortly after delivery.
(courtesy T. Varley)

252. Yorkshire No 44, their
first steam wagon, seen in a
ditch at Horley, Surrey on 14th
April 1904.
(author's collection)

253. A scene on the main road outside Bentley's Yorkshire Brewery at Woodlesford, Leeds *circa* 1905. On the left of the photograph is Yorkshire No 56, Registration No C 465, built in February 1904 and the fleet No 1. In the centre is Yorkshire No 80, Registration No C 960, and built in April 1904, fleet No 3. Completing the trio is a Mann wagon, Registration No C 520, fitted with dual steering controls.

(courtesy D.A. Rayner)

254. Yorkshire 4 ton undertype wagon No 56, Registration No C 465, was built in February 1902 and sold to Bentley's Yorkshire Breweries of Woodesford, where she became No 1 in their fleet, probably replacing a pair of shire horses.

(courtesy D.A. Rayner)

255.   Yorkshire 6 ton undertype wagon No 205, Registration No U 361, was built in September 1907 and sold to Sharphouse & Company of Lofthousegate, Yorkshire. When built she was given a 5 ton type boiler but in August 1908 received a new 6 ton type boiler and by January 1921 she had been sold to Stephen Smart of Carbrook, Sheffield. This photograph shows her trying to enter a Pork butcher's shop at Worsborough, near Barnsley: the date of this incident is not recorded. (courtesy T. Varley)

256.   Spectators take the opportunity to inspect this unfamiliar aspect of a steam wagon. The unfortunate vehicle is Yorkshire 6 ton undertype wagon No 215, Registration No U 785, which overturned after running off the road and crashing through a stone wall. Built in January 1908, she was sold to an owner in Brighouse in Yorkshire and had two more Yorkshire owners before being sold in 1921 to Moody & Liddicoat of Bicester, Oxfordshire. Unfortunately there are no other details accompanying this old photograph. (courtesy R.G. Pratt)

257.   Yorkshire 6 ton undertype wagon No 342, Registration No U 1769, was built in March 1912 and sold to Stephen Gilks of Shaw, Lancashire. In 1921 the firm became Butterworth & Gilks and by 1929 the wagon had been sold for scrap. (courtesy T. Varley)

258. Yorkshire 6 ton undertype tipping wagon No 587, Registration No U 2135, was built in March 1913 and sold to James Robinson & Son (Sheffield) Ltd. By October 1924 she had been sold to Sheffield Corporation and became their fleet No 70. She was last licenced in December 1936. *(courtesy T. Varley)*

259. Yorkshire 6 ton tipping wagon No 745, Registration No U 3541, was built in November 1915 and sold to the Stretford & District Gas Board, Lancashire. *(courtesy T. Varley)*

260.   Yorkshire GF series 6 ton undertype wagon No 1377, Registration No BB 7378, was built in July 1923. Fitted with a gully emptier she was supplied to Newcastle-upon-Tyne Corporation where she became No 18 in their fleet.   *(courtesy T. Varley)*

261.   Yorkshire 5/6 ton undertype tipping wagon No 1506, Registration No WT 9823, was built in April 1925 and sold to Doncaster Rural District Council (later the West Riding County Council) where she became No 4 in their fleet. In 1936 she was sold as scrap to E. Sheard of Wakefield.   *(courtesy T. Varley)*

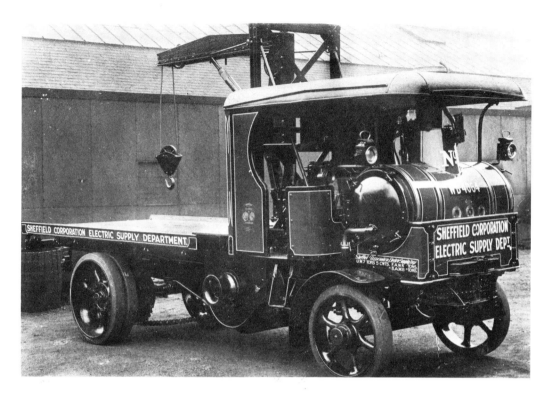

262 & 263.   Yorkshire 6 ton WE series undertype wagon No 1526, Registration No WB 4064, was built in October 1925 and sold to Sheffield Corporation Electricity Department where she became No 1 in their fleet. She was last licenced in March 1932. In the lower photograph a 3¼ ton capacity crane is shown being demonstrated with nearly 3½ tons being lifted.

(courtesy T. Varley)

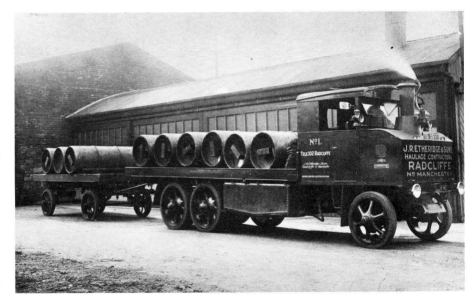

264. Yorkshire WJ series 10/15 ton undertype wagon No 2150, Registration No CE 5690, was built in November 1928 and sold to J.R. Etheridge & Son of Radcliffe, Lancashire, where she became No 1 in their fleet.
(courtesy T. Varley)

265. Yorkshire WJ series 10/15 ton undertype wagon No 2153, Registration No KP 3629, was built in July 1929 and sold to British Standard Cement Co Ltd (E.J. & W. Goldsmith Ltd) of Rainham, Kent where she became No 115 in their fleet.
(courtesy T. Varley)

266. Yorkshire WJ series 10/15 ton undertype wagon No 2160, Registration No GU 6281, was built in April 1929 and sold to the Cement Marketing Company Ltd, London, where she became No 57 in their fleet.
(courtesy T. Varley)

267. Yorkshire WM series undertype chassis and cab, No 2173, Registration No UR 5716, was built in January 1930 and supplied to McMullen & Sons Ltd, of Hertford. *(courtesy T. Varley)*

268. Yorkshire WG series undertype wagon No 2176 fitted with a gully emptier. She carried Registration No PG 6958 and was built in March 1930 for Reigate Corporation, Surrey where she became No 5 in their fleet. *(courtesy T. Varley)*